D1785616

WHSmith

Practise

Writing and Punctuation

KS2 ENGLISH

Age 7–9

Brenda Stones

Advice for parents

These days we are expected to be able to write fluently either by hand or on a keyboard, depending on the purpose of our writing. This book therefore gives lots of practice in writing activities, to help children think and plan, imagine and create through their writing. It can be daunting to start writing on a blank page, so these pages are devised to give your child the starting points and building blocks to get them writing. Extra paper should be available for longer writing tasks.

There is a whole range of writing forms represented in the book, from lists and adverts, through letters and playscripts, to short stories and poems. These are all forms of writing that children cover in Years 3–4 at primary school: the first half of the book being non-fictional forms, and the second half fictional.

Practising and checking punctuation is deliberately integrated within the writing tasks, rather than being taught separately, out of context.

- On the left-hand side of each double page is a model of a particular form of writing, to remind your child of the style, layout and punctuation of that form.
- On the right-hand side is space for your child to write their own piece in a similar style. But encourage your child to use their imagination and think of their own content, characters and contexts for writing. These are 'open-ended' tasks, so that each child can write to their own level of ability.
- Each unit ends with a further suggestion for writing that your child can do away from the book.
- The book ends with a quiz, to round up what your child has learnt.
- And finally we provide answers, to help either parents or children to check their work.

The most important thing is for your child to enjoy writing: it is a skill and a pleasure they will use throughout their lives!

First published 2007
exclusively for WHSmith by
Hodder Murray, a member of the Hodder Headline group
338 Euston Road
London
NW1 3BH

Impression number   10 9 8 7 6 5 4 3 2 1
Year   2008 2007
Text and illustrations © Hodder Education 2007

All rights reserved. No part of this publication may be reproduced or transmitted in any form or by any means, electronic or mechanical, including photocopying, recording or any information storage and retrieval system, without permission in writing from the publisher.

A CIP record for this book is available from the British Library.

Cover illustration: Sally Newton Illustrations
Character illustrations: Beehive Illustration
All other illustrations: Simon Dennett at SD Illustration, Arthur Pickering and Kelly Gray
Typeset by Florence Production Ltd, Stoodleigh, Devon

ISBN – 13   978 0 304 94339 7

Printed and bound in Scotland

Contents

Welcome to Kids Club!

Hi, readers. My name's Charlie and I run Kids Club with my friend Abbie. Kids Club is an after-school club which is very similar to one somewhere near you.

We'd love you to come and join our club and see what we get up to!

I'm Abbie. Let's meet the kids who will work with you on the activities in this book.

My name's Jamelia. I look forward to Kids Club every day. The sports and games are my favourites, especially on Kids Camp in the school holidays.

Hi, I'm Megan. I've made friends with all the kids at Kids Club. I like the outings and trips we go on the best.

Hello, my name's Kim. Kids Club is a great place to chill out after school. My best friend is Alfie – he's a bit naughty but he means well!

I'm Amina. I like to do my homework at Kids Club. Charlie and Abbie are always very helpful. We're like one big happy family.

Greetings, readers, my name's Alfie! Everybody knows me here. Come and join our club; we'll have a wicked time together!

Now you've met us all, tell us something about yourself.
All the kids filled in a '**Personal Profile**' when they joined. Here's one for you to complete.

Personal Profile

INSERT PHOTO OF YOURSELF HERE

Name: _____

Age: _____

School: _____

Home town: _____

Best friend: _____

My favourite:

● Book _____

● Film _____

● Food _____

● Sport _____

My hero is _____ because _____

_____

When I grow up I want to be a _____

If I ruled the world the first thing I would do is _____

_____

If I could be any celebrity for a day I would be _____

_____

1: Write a list

Here's a list that Megan wrote. It lists all her favourite things in life. They are all the things she'd save if there was a flood!

My pink boots

My old teddy bear

My gran's photo

My first tooth

My black mouse

My diary

Big bottle of water for survival

My mobile

My purple pen

The chocolate cake from my last birthday party

Get ready

1 Do you use capital letters in this kind of list?

_____

2 Do you use punctuation in this kind of list?

_____

3 When do you start a new line in a list?

_____

Let's practise

Now write a list of the ten things you'd save, if you knew a mega-disaster was coming!

Never mind if some of them are a bit difficult to pack . . .

1
2
3
4
5
6
7
8
9
10

Have a go

Go and ask other people in your family what they'd save, and make lists for each of them.

2: Write a recipe

A recipe is a kind of **instruction**, which tells you how to make something.

It's often a recipe for cooking, but it might be for making something else.

Here's a recipe that's really different.

How to make your mum happy

You will need:

1 piece of card   1 tray   Your mum's favourite food and drink

What to do:

1 Fold the card and draw a picture on the front.
2 Write a message inside, telling your mum what a great person she is.
3 Find a tray in the kitchen, or a very strong piece of board.
4 Pile on her favourite food and drink.
5 Find a good moment when she's sitting down.
6 Give her the tray and your card as a big surprise.
7 Last of all, give her a big kiss!

Get ready

What are the headings for the two parts of the instruction?

1 _____

2 _____

Let's practise

Now think up your own idea for a recipe in life.

It could be how to make your best friend happy, or it could be how to make a really awful mess!

You will need:

_____

_____

_____

What to do:

1 _____

2 _____

3 _____

4 _____

Write down the recipe for cooking your favourite food.

First list the things you need, then list the things you do to make the dish. Make your instructions as clear as possible.

3: Write directions

Another kind of instruction tells someone how to get somewhere.

This is called giving **directions**, and it helps if you have a map to work from.

Here are the directions that Little Red Riding Hood's mother gave her to reach her grandmother's house in the woods.

Leave the house behind you, and walk straight on for half a mile.
When you come to the big oak tree, turn right.
Walk on another half a mile until you come to the stream.
Cross the bridge, and turn left.
When you reach the ruined farm, turn right.
Grandmother's house is then straight in front of you.

Get ready

Draw a line on the picture to show where Little Red Riding Hood had to go. Start from the house at the bottom.

Let's practise

Write the directions that Grandmother would have given Little Red Riding Hood to get back home. That is, if she hadn't been eaten by the wolf . . .

_____

_____

_____

_____

_____

_____

_____

_____

_____

Have a go

Write directions for your best friend, telling him or her how to get from school to your home. You could draw a map as well, if it helps.

4: Write a definition

When do you use a dictionary?

A dictionary is really useful for checking your spelling, and for finding out what words mean.

The meaning of a word is also called a **definition**.

Read the definitions below. Fill in the word you think each definition is describing on the first line.

_____ a large monster with wings, that you read about in stories _____

_____ a very big piece of ice floating in the sea _____

_____ a word describing the taste of nuts _____

_____ a person whose job is to fit and mend water pipes and taps _____

_____ to go backwards in a car _____

Get ready

1. Look up the words in your own dictionary. Which definition do you prefer: the one above or the one in your dictionary?

2. Now write **noun**, **verb** or **adjective** after each word. Your dictionary may tell you this.

Let's practise

Now try writing your own definitions for these words:

deckchair _____

_____

haunted _____

_____

magnet _____

_____

nose _____

_____

rise _____

_____

sword _____

_____

wand _____

_____

Have a go

Play a game reading definitions from the dictionary and asking your friends to guess what the words are.

5: Write an advert

How do you persuade someone that they'd like what you like?

You have to be very good with words to describe something so that you make someone else want to try it too.

Take your favourite food, for instance – how can you turn a yummy taste into the kind of description that makes your best friend beg for a bite?

WHEN YOU'VE CRUNCHED THROUGH THE MUNCHY BIT, AND SUCKED UP THE SOFTY BIT, THE RICH BIT IN THE MIDDLE IS THE MELTING CHOCOLATE CENTRE OF THE PERFECT CHOCOLATE DOUGHNUT. IT'S A CHOCOHOLIC'S DREAM COME TRUE!

Get ready

Find a highlighter pen, and mark each word in the advert that really tempts you.

Let's practise

Describe your favourite food, and draw a picture, to make us all want a taste.

Have a go

Invent a new toy, and write an advert persuading parents to buy it for their children. Draw a picture, too, if you like.

6: Write a questionnaire

Do you like asking questions? If so, you could try writing a questionnaire for friends and family to fill in.

Here's one that Megan wrote, with the answers she got from her granny.

What is your name?	Granny Ross
What is your favourite food?	Baked beans
What is your favourite colour?	Purple
Where was your favourite holiday?	Wales
Who is your favourite singer?	Billy Fury
What is your favourite animal?	Giraffe
What are your favourite shoes?	My fur boots
What time do you go to bed?	Never before 10 o'clock

Get ready

1 List the question words used at the start of the sentences.

_____

2 What is put at the end of each question? _____

3 What punctuation is used in the answers? _____

Let's practise

Now write your own questionnaire, for your friends or family.

You could add lots of different questions, like: What is the earliest thing you can remember happening to you?

_____

_____

_____

_____

_____

_____

_____

_____

Have a go

Make copies of your questionnaire, if you can, so you can ask lots of different people to fill in their answers.

7: Write a letter

When do we write letters? When we want to tell someone something, and maybe when we don't know someone well enough to telephone or text.

Have you ever written to an author, to tell them how much you like their book?

This is the letter I typed to Robert Swindells to tell him how much I enjoyed reading his book *Ice Palace*.

---

26 Sunny Terrace
Chelmsford CO5 9AH

26 August 2007

Dear Mr Swindells,

I'd like to tell you how much I enjoyed reading Ice Palace.

I found the whole book a wonderful fantasy story, which made me feel really scared, as well as wanting to read on to the end.

The bit I especially liked was when Ivan was stuck in the cave, and searching for his brother.

Thank you for writing this book. I shall try to find more of your stories in our library.

Yours sincerely,
Amina Desai

Get ready

Can you find all these parts of the letter? Draw lines to link them to the text above.

1 Home address

2 Date

3 Greeting

4 Message

5 Ending

Let's practise

Write a letter to your favourite author. Tell them which is your favourite book of theirs, why you liked the book overall, what your favourite bit was, and what you might read next.

_____

_____

_____

_____

_____

_____

_____

_____

_____

Have a go

Write a letter to your local library, asking them to stock a book you've really enjoyed.

8: Explain in words

I'm fascinated by how things are made, or how things get to where they are.

We often use pictures or diagrams to show how these things happen.

Can you see what the pictures below are telling us?

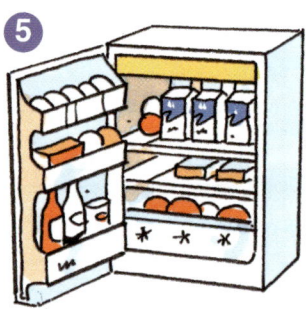

Get ready

1. Talk through what's happening in the pictures, as if the person you're talking to doesn't understand them.

2. Did you notice which tense you were using? Was it the present tense or the past tense?

 **Let's practise**

Now write down your explanation in words.

Use the numbered stages to help you.

1 _____

_____

2 _____

_____

3 _____

_____

4 _____

_____

5 _____

_____

6 _____

_____

 **Have a go**

Write out the explanation of how something else is made.

Try drawing the pictures as well, if you can.

Do you ever read newspapers, to read **reports** of things that have happened?

If the report describes the events in the order that they happened, it is called a **chronological report**.

Look at the newspaper report below, which describes an escape from a zoo.

PYTHON ESCAPES!

Fear and panic swept the town of Marwick as a mountain python escaped from its cage.

The keepers first noticed it was missing at dawn, when they went round with morning feeds. They raised the alarm, and local police were given instructions on how to corner the snake, if anyone reported a sighting.

Early in the day the local school reported a possible sighting, but the zoo were not sure if they believed the stripy creature spotted in the playground really was the python.

Residents at an old people's home then thought they'd seen something slithery, but again it disappeared before the police could follow it.

In the end the zoo found the python in the farm area, where it had eaten all the rabbits and mice. So maybe it had never got out into the town at all.

Get ready

① What tense is the main report written in, the past tense or the present tense? _____

② Can you spot all the words that mark the sequence of time (connecting words), at the beginning of each paragraph? Mark them with a highlighter pen.

Now write a newspaper report of a dramatic incident in your home town.

Use the past tense, and use connecting words at the beginning of each paragraph, to stress the sequence of time.

Write a report for your school newspaper or school website, describing an event that happened at school.

10: Write your point of view

Suppose you wanted to respond to that newspaper article about the python escaping. Imagine you thought the zoo should think more about safety in your school and neighbourhood. Here's the kind of letter you might write.

Primrose School
Princess Road
Marwick MAR 6JL

1 October 2007

Dear Marwick Zoo,

We were worried to read in the local newspaper that one of your pythons might have escaped last week.

We kept thinking we'd seen it in the playground, so we were very scared.

We think it's important for the local neighbourhood to feel safe, so we hope that you have enough guards to make sure your animals don't escape.

We'd like to hear more about how your zoo is run.

Yours sincerely,
Class 4B

Get ready

1. Compare this letter with the one in Unit 7. Which features do the newspaper article and letter have in common?

   _____

2. What were the class worried about?

   _____

3. How did they make the letter end on a positive note?

   _____

Let's practise

Now write your own letter to the zoo, expressing a different point of view. Maybe you think they shouldn't be keeping pythons there at all. Make sure you lay out the letter in the same way as the one from Class 4B.

_____

_____

_____

_____

_____

_____

_____

_____

_____

Have a go

Look through your local newspaper for reports that make you want to respond. Write a letter to the newspaper giving your point of view.

11: Write a playscript

Do you know what a playscript is?

A **playscript** is how we write out the words that people speak in a play.

Look at this example, and read the different speeches out loud.

[*The* MAYOR *is sitting with his* COUNCILLORS.]

MAYOR: What on earth are we going to do? Our town is overrun with rats!

1st COUNCILLOR: There are rats in the cellars!

2nd COUNCILLOR: There are rats in the streets!

[*Enter a young man, dressed in red and yellow.*]

PIED PIPER: Please, sirs. I think I can help you.

MAYOR: How can you do that?

PIED PIPER: I know a charm that makes animals follow me.

MAYOR: And how do you do that?

PIED PIPER: I play on this pipe, and the animals follow.

MAYOR: That's wonderful! What should we pay you?

PIED PIPER: [*Modestly*] I'd like a thousand gilders, please.

MAYOR: We'll give you fifty thousand gilders, sir!

Get ready

Now match each of these features to the script above, by drawing lines to examples in the text.

1. Name of the person speaking, in capitals

2. Words the people say, in ordinary type

3. Stage directions, in square brackets and italics

Try writing a part of a playscript.

You could choose a well-known folk tale, like the one here. Or you could use a story you make up yourself.

Include all the features from the example opposite. You will need to continue on a separate piece of paper.

_____

_____

_____

_____

_____

_____

_____

_____

Act out your playscript with a group of friends.

12: Punctuate speech

In the last unit, we looked at how to write speech in a play.
If you are writing speech in a cartoon strip or in a story, you do it differently.
Below, we're going to show you the same story of the Pied Piper, first as a cartoon, and then as a story.

The Mayor was sitting with his Councillors, and he was very worried.
"What on earth are we going to do?" he asked. "Our town is overrun with rats!"
"There are rats in the cellars!" said the First Councillor.
"There are rats in the streets!" echoed the Second Councillor.
At that point a young man came in, dressed in red and yellow.
"Please, sirs," he said softly. "I think I can help you."
The Mayor was amazed. "How can you do that?" he asked.
"I know a charm that makes animals follow me," said the Piper.

When do you use speech marks to show the words people speak?
Mark with a tick (✓) or a cross (✗).

1 Playscript ☐   **2** Speech bubbles ☐   **3** Story ☐

Let's practise

Take the playscript you wrote in Unit 11.

Write it out as a story, using the model opposite for how to do the speech marks.
Look at the model carefully – it's quite fiddly, putting the speech marks and the other punctuation in the right places. You will need to continue on a separate piece of paper.

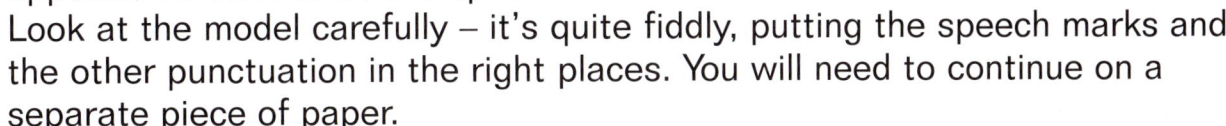

_____

_____

_____

_____

_____

_____

_____

_____

_____

Have a go

Draw the same conversation as a cartoon with speech bubbles.

13: Write a character sketch

Can you describe someone so that your reader can really picture him or her?

Can you make your reader either want to meet the person or run a mile?

You have to describe all the little details of what people look like and how they might behave, if you are to make your reader really believe in them!

Here is a **character sketch**.

I saw someone walking their dog this morning.

At least, first I just saw the dog-lead in the gap of our front hedge. So I started to imagine who was on each end of the dog-lead, before I caught a full picture of the two of them.

It was the dog I saw first. He was one of those pit bull terriers who look rather scary, but are probably quite amiable really. He had big square shoulders, and rather turned-out feet.

He was moving slowly, as if he was not out for a walk so much as ambling out to inspect the neighbourhood. He had slitty eyes, as if he hadn't quite woken up yet.

So it wasn't such a surprise when the owner then appeared in the next gap of the hedge. He was slow on his feet too. And his toes turned out too. He wasn't menacing at all, more just a sleepy character who liked to look a bit more frightening than he really was. I then remembered that I'd seen them both in the park, the dog asleep on the ground with his legs splayed out, and the man asleep on a bench, in the middle of the afternoon.

They left me thinking: which came first, the man or the dog?

① Read the character sketch, and use a highlighter pen to mark the bits you think the writer has done best.

② Are there any words you don't know? Either try guessing what they mean, or look them up in a dictionary.

Let's practise

Try writing your own character sketch of a dog and its owner. Really try to picture them in your head. Don't forget to use lots of details to describe their appearance, and what this suggests about how they might behave.

_____

_____

_____

_____

_____

_____

_____

_____

Have a go

Look for a photo in a magazine of someone whose life you'd like to imagine. Try writing a day-in-the-life of your character.

14: Describe a setting

Where do stories happen? Where would you like to make a story of yours happen?

You need to use lots of adjectives to describe your setting, so that your reader can picture it exactly.

Deep in a dark black space. Dank and dark, bleak and black. Is there any light at all? Yes, there's a piercing white light ahead: could it be the mouth of a cave, or the light at the end of a tunnel? It's a tiny relief compared with this overwhelming blackness, this damp chilling darkness, enveloping everything. What are the sounds? A drip of moisture from the roof, falling into a puddle in the rough ground underfoot. But otherwise there is just silence, leaving me nothing to hear, as well as nothing to see. Where on earth am I?

Get ready

1   Highlight all the adjectives in the description above.

2   Do you think the description is effective? _____

_____

Let's practise

Now it's your turn to describe a setting.
Will you make it obvious where it is?
Or will you leave your reader guessing?
Don't forget your adjectives, and think
of all the senses you use: sight,
hearing, touch, taste and smell.

_____

_____

_____

_____

_____

_____

_____

_____

Have a go

Again, try looking through a magazine, this time to find somewhere
gorgeous you'd like to go on holiday. Describe what you think the place
would be like.

Now you can start to plan a whole story, using your character in your setting. (Or choose a new character in a new setting.)

What's going to happen? You need a **beginning**, a **middle** and an **ending** to make your plot work. Look at the plan below.

Character
Man and dog

Setting
Dark tunnel

Beginning
They wake up

Middle
They realise where they are

Ending
They walk to safety

Get ready

Would you plan your character and your setting completely before you begin to plan your plot? Or do you think they might develop while you are writing?

_____

 **Let's practise**

Fill in the boxes below to plan your own story.

When you come to write your story, you will write a paragraph each for the **beginning**, **middle** and **ending**.

Character	Setting
_____	_____

Beginning

_____

_____

Middle

_____

_____

Ending

_____

_____

 **Have a go**

When you are ready, get a separate piece of paper and write your story. This is just your rough draft. You will write your final version a bit later . . .

In the last unit we planned our stories, and you went off to write a rough version of your whole plot.

Here's what we wrote for the three paragraphs of our plot.

The man woke up slowly. Where on earth was he? It was pitch black, and rather damp. At least the dog was still at his feet; that was something. But what were they doing here?
He stroked his dog's familiar fur, to stop himself trembling with panic.

"Come on, boy," he said. "We've got to get out of here."
They headed towards the source of light, stumbling through the puddles.
"If only the dog could talk," he thought. "He could remind me how we got in here."
They headed forwards, the man keeping one hand on the side of the tunnel for safety. The shape of the light got bigger and bigger, in the shape of a growing white 'n'.

At last they broke into the daylight. They were on the bank of a little canal, which snaked round the hillside to bring water to all the crops. They had been inside one of the tunnels the canal flowed through, and the man must have fallen or passed out while they were in the tunnel. Never again! He would make sure he never walked through dark tunnels again for the rest of his life!

Get ready

When you've read the story, have a look at the punctuation.

1   Does every sentence start with a capital letter and end with either a full stop, a question mark or an exclamation mark? Mark them all in red.

2   Has the author used commas to separate a list, or to help the reader pause in the middle of a sentence? Mark the commas in blue.

3   Has the author used any semi-colons and colons in the middle of sentences for longer pauses? Mark them in pink.

4   Has the author used speech marks correctly for speech? Mark them in green.

Let's practise

Now you can 'edit' your rough version of your story, by checking the four punctuation questions in **Get ready**.

When you are ready, copy out a final version of your story into the space below. You may need to continue on a separate piece of paper.

Have a go

Try writing a longer story, of more than three paragraphs. You could then make it into a folded book, with a proper cover, and give it to someone in your family as a present.

17: Write a different ending

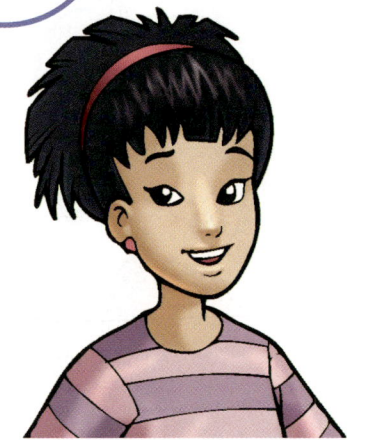

Do you remember the setting and characters we brought together in Unit 15?

Well, maybe there's a different explanation of how the man and his dog got into the tunnel, and how they'll get out!

Here's a spider diagram with lots of different possibilities.

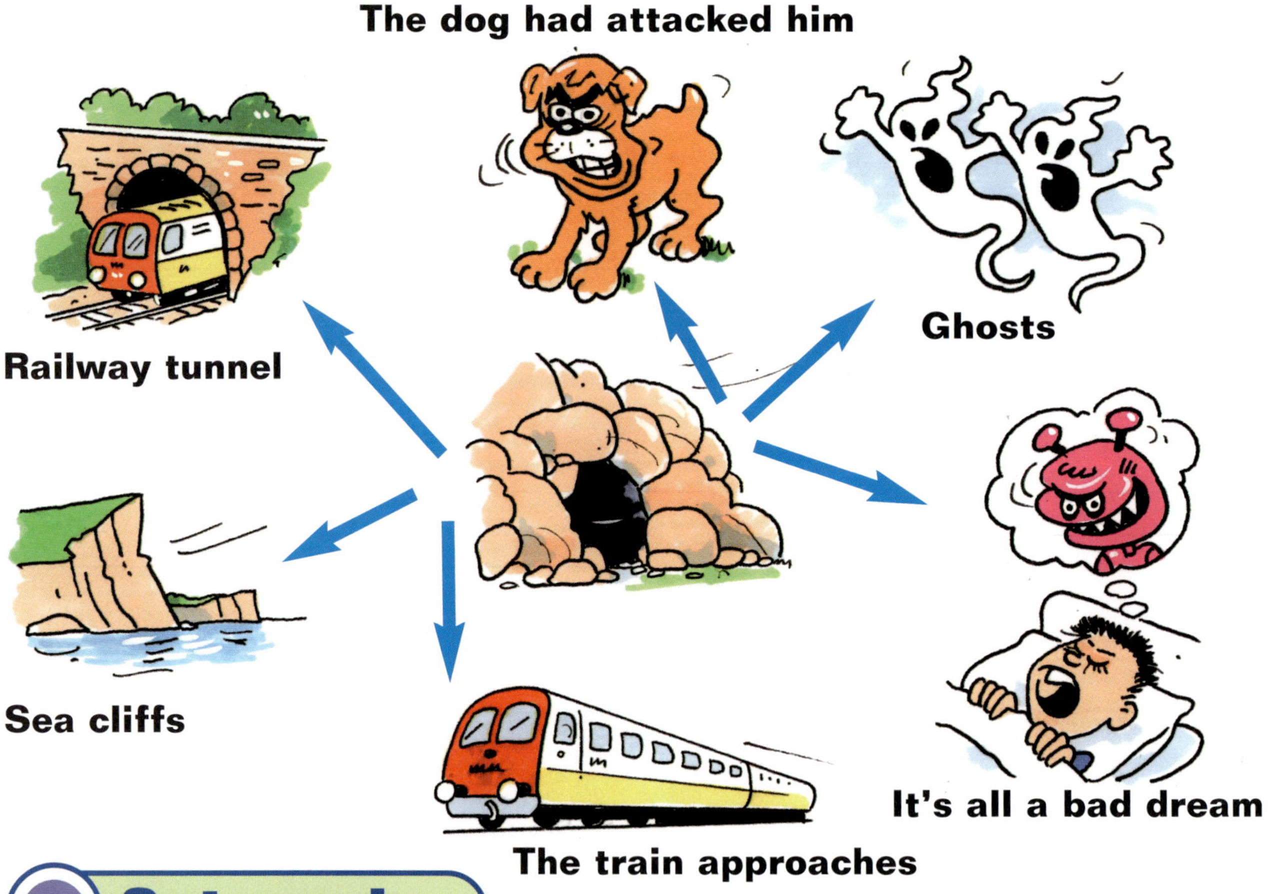
The dog had attacked him
Ghosts
Railway tunnel
It's all a bad dream
Sea cliffs
The train approaches

Get ready

Mark the spider diagram with ticks (✓), crosses (✗) and question marks (?) to indicate how you feel about each possibility.

Which option was your favourite?

Or would you choose something entirely different from your own imagination?

Write a different ending to the story, to make it more exciting for you. You may need to continue on a separate piece of paper.

_____

_____

_____

_____

_____

_____

_____

_____

Have a go

Take a well-known story, and write a completely different ending for it.

Does your ending make the story better?

18: Write a poem

Write a whole poem myself! How scary does that sound?

Actually there are lots of ways of making it less scary. One way is to work from a 'model'. This means you look at the form or shape of someone else's poem, and use it as a 'prompt' to write your own. And that's quite all right – it's not cheating.

So, read aloud the poem below.

My Week at School

On Monday we did pottery,
On Tuesday we did craft;
On Wednesday we did sums and things,
On Thursday we just laughed.
On Friday we did question marks,
And What and Why and Who,
But now that it's the weekend
I can choose just what I'll do!

Get ready

Which lines rhyme? Number the lines, and draw lines to link the ones that rhyme.

Let's practise

Try using the same idea, of the days of the week, to write your own poem.

Look out for which lines have to rhyme!

On Monday _____

On Tuesday _____

On Wednesday _____

On Thursday _____

On Friday _____

_____

_____

_____

Have a go

Try using times of day, or the months of the year, as a way of shaping some more poems.

Do you like shape poems? I love reading them, but I've never tried writing one before.

One way of doing it is to draw the shape of a country or continent and then, inside the shape, write all the words that the place makes you think of.

Here's one on Africa, for instance.

ochre   terracotta
apricot   bronze
scorching   baking
burning   dry   desert
deserted   dusty
music beating
dancing
heartland
motherland

Africa

Get ready

What colours does this poem make you think of? Colour in the shape with the right kind of colours.

Let's practise

Now write a shape poem of your own. It doesn't have to be about a country; it could be about a food, or a building, or a person. Draw the outline shape first, and then fill it with words that the shape makes you think of.

Have a go

Write shape poems for a whole jungle full of wild animals!

20: Write a haiku

Now let's try a **haiku**.

A haiku has three lines, with the middle line longer than the first and last.

Here are some examples.

a

An old pond
The sound of a frog jumping
Into water.

b

First day of school
Toes cramped and blistered red
From new school shoes.

c

Last day of term
Classroom chairs looking forward to
Weeks of peace.

Get ready

How many syllables are there in each line of the three haiku above? Many haiku have five, seven and five syllables in their three lines, but not all haiku follow this pattern.

Let's practise

Now try writing your own haiku.

Haiku are often about the seasons, so that might help to get you started.

One author has recently tried condensing the plots of major novels into haiku. Could you do this for your favourite novel?

Quiz on writing

Can you remember which special features you'd find in these different kinds of writing?

Draw lines to match them up.

What you need:	Instructions
Turn left.	Character sketch
Address and date	Questionnaire
What's your name?	Speech
PIED PIPER:	Playscript
[*He came in slowly*.]	Recipe
"Too right," he said.	Directions
Poem of three lines	Setting
He was a burly man.	Haiku
It was a dark and stormy night.	Letter

Careful! It's not necessarily one feature per kind of writing . . .

Quiz on punctuation

Each of these lines has an error of punctuation.

Write out the correct version on the line below.

1 "All right" said the clown.

_____

2 I'll take all these the ball the ring and the crown.

_____

3 The bird, which was sitting on the line sang the loudest.

_____

4 How on earth can I handle all that.

_____

5 "Are we going to school?" She asked.

_____

6 William said. "It's just as well."

_____

7 You take the shortest; We'll take the longest.

_____

8 It's about time too, I replied.

_____

9 Those were the days she said, with a sigh.

_____

10 And that's all for now I'm afraid.

_____

Answers

Unit 1 (pages 6 and 7)
1 Yes, for each new line
2 No
3 For each new item

Unit 2 (pages 8 and 9)
1 You will need:
2 What to do:

Unit 4 (pages 12 and 13)
dragon, noun
iceberg, noun
nutty, adjective
plumber, noun
reverse, verb

Unit 6 (pages 16 and 17)
1 What, Where, Who
2 Question mark
3 Only capital letter, no full stop

Unit 8 (pages 20 and 21)
2 Present tense

Unit 9 (pages 22 and 23)
1 Past tense
2 first, Early in the day, then, In the end

Unit 10 (pages 24 and 25)
1 Address, Date, Greeting, Message, Ending
2 Their safety
3 Asking about how the zoo is run

Unit 12 (pages 28 and 29)
1 Playscript (✗)
2 Speech bubbles (✗)
3 Story (✓)

Unit 14 (pages 32 and 33)
1 Deep, dark, black, Dank, dark, bleak, black, piercing, white, tiny, overwhelming, damp, chilling, rough

Unit 15 (pages 34 and 35)
Child's own answer

Unit 16 (pages 36 and 37)
The man woke up slowly. Where on earth was he? It was pitch black, and rather damp. At least the dog was still at his feet; that was something. But what were they doing here?

He stroked his dog's familiar fur, to stop himself trembling with panic.

"Come on, boy," he said. "We've got to get out of here."

They headed towards the source of light, stumbling through the puddles.

"If only the dog could talk," he thought. "He could remind me how we got in here."

They headed forwards, the man keeping one hand on the side of the tunnel for safety. The shape of the light got bigger and bigger, in the shape of a growing white 'n'.

At last they broke into the daylight. They were on the bank of a little canal, which snaked round the hillside to bring water to all the crops. They had been inside one of the tunnels the canal flowed through, and he must have fallen or passed out while they were in the tunnel. Never again! He would make sure he never walked through dark tunnels again for the rest of his life!

Unit 18 (pages 40 and 41)
Lines 2 and 4, and lines 6 and 8

Unit 20 (pages 44 and 45)
a 3, 7, 4
b 4, 6, 4
c 4, 8, 3

How have I done? (pages 46 and 47)
Quiz on writing
What you need: . . . . .Recipe / Instructions
Turn left . . . . .Directions
Address and date . . . . .Letter
What's your name? . . . . .Questionnaire
PIED PIPER: . . . . .Playscript
[He came in slowly.] . . . . .Playscript
"Too right," he said . . . . .Speech
Poem of three lines . . . . .Haiku
He was a burly man . . . . .Character sketch
It was a dark and stormy night . . . .Setting

Quiz on punctuation
1 "All right," said the clown.
2 I'll take all these: the ball, the ring and the crown.
3 The bird, which was sitting on the line, sang the loudest.
4 How on earth can I handle all that?
5 "Are we going to school?" she asked.
6 William said, "It's just as well."
7 You take the shortest; we'll take the longest.
8 "It's about time too," I replied.
9 "Those were the days," she said, with a sigh.
10 And that's all for now, I'm afraid.
 or And that's all. For now I'm afraid.